FRIENDSHIP, DATING, AND RELATIONSHIPS

Simone Payment

ROSEN
PUBLISHING®

New York

Published in 2010 by The Rosen Publishing Group, Inc.
29 East 21st Street, New York, NY 10010

Library of Congress Cataloging-in-Publication Data

Payment, Simone.
Friendship, dating, and relationships / Simone Payment.—1st ed.
    p. cm.—(Teens: being gay, lesbian, bisexual, or transgender)
Includes bibliographical references and index.
ISBN 978-1-4358-3578-8 (library binding)
1. Teenagers—Sexual behavior—Juvenile literature. 2. Gays—Juvenile
literature. 3. Gender identity—Juvenile literature. 4. Interpersonal relations—
Juvenile literature. I. Title.
HQ27.P378 2010
306.76—dc22

                                                                2009014866

Manufactured in Malaysia

CPSIA Compliance information: Batch #TW10YA: For Further Information contact Rosen Publishing, New York, New York

at 1-800-237-9932

CONTENTS

Introduction

You may be reading this book because you already know you're gay, lesbian, bisexual, or transgender (GLBT). Maybe you have a friend or sibling who is GLBT and want more information. Or maybe you're wondering if you might be GLBT but aren't sure.

Part of being a young adult is questioning who you are as a person. What are you good at? What kind of friend are you? What do you like to do in your spare time? What kind of career do you want to pursue? Naturally, this process of self-discovery also includes what kind of person you're attracted to and what kind of person you think you could fall in love with. Answers to many of these questions don't come right away. You might not have definitive answers in two weeks or two years—or even twenty years. People are always changing, and finding these answers is an evolving process.

Introduction

This book explores the relationships that GLBT teens have with themselves, their friends, and with people they might choose to date. Dating and relationships are an important part of the teen years, and it's normal to have lots of questions. For GLBT teens, these questions may be different from those of their straight counterparts. Sometimes, it can be difficult to get answers. Even well-meaning, sympathetic parents and siblings may have difficulty answering questions about GLBT relationships.

Rest assured, there are answers. If you are a GLBT teen, you are not alone. Many other people have had similar experiences, questions, and worries. There are many people and organizations that can help you sort through your feelings and find answers to your questions. If you are a GLBT teen, it doesn't mean there is something wrong with you. Being GLBT is not something you need to change. In fact, it is not something you *can* change. Over time, society has become more accepting of these facts, and more and more teens feel comfortable acknowledging that they are GLBT.

In this book, we'll discuss what it means to be GLBT. We'll talk about the process of coming out, or telling your family and friends that you are GLBT. We'll discuss the importance of friendships, and you'll also find information about where to meet other GLBT teens. If you're thinking about dating, this book can help you decide if you are ready. If you are already dating, this book discusses potential problems or hazards you might encounter, and how to deal with the end of a relationship.

CHAPTER 1

Your Relationship with Yourself

Thinking about your sexual orientation or gender identity can be scary and confusing, but it can also be exciting and rewarding. It's important that you be patient with yourself. No one says you have to know everything about yourself at age fifteen, eighteen, or even thirty-five. Think things through, and get as much information as you can to help you along the way.

Remember that there is no "right" answer to your questions about your sexual identity. Sexual orientations, such as straight, gay, lesbian, bisexual, and transgender, are all normal varieties of human sexuality. Not all people think that being GLBT is normal, so some people may be less accepting of those who are GLBT. However, medical and psychological organizations like the American Academy of Pediatrics, the American Psychological Association, and the National Association of Social Workers agree that if you are GLBT, you are just like anyone else. Being GLBT is perfectly normal.

What Is GLBT?

"GLBT" is an acronym for gay, lesbian, bisexual, or transgender. "Gay" is a general term used to describe men who are attracted to other men, although it can also be used to describe anyone who is attracted to members of the same sex. Lesbians are women who are attracted to other women. Bisexuals can be attracted to men and women. Transgender people may find that their biological sex does not match their gender identity. A person's sex, whether it is male or female, is based on biological characteristics. A person's gender is based on whether he or she feels male or female. The gender that a person identifies with is known as his or her gender identity. A transgender person might identify as a woman, but have been born biologically male. The way that a person manifests or exhibits his or her gender is known as gender expression.

Gender includes traditional ideas of how men or women are supposed to look and behave, how they are supposed to dress, and what they are supposed to enjoy. For example, men were once expected to wear pants, like sports, and have short hair. Women were once expected to wear dresses, enjoy cooking, and have long hair. Over time, however, traditional gender expectations have changed. For example, today it's perfectly acceptable to most people if women have short hair and like sports, and if men like cooking and have long hair.

Many colleges and universities now offer classes on GLBT topics and issues. This professor at San Francisco State University conducts a class on GLBT cultures.

For people who are transgender, their biological sex and their gender identity do not match. Transgender people may feel that their body just does not correspond with how they feel on the inside, or with how they want to act or dress. For example, as a child, a transgender person born female may have felt uncomfortable when her parents dressed her in a skirt. She may have preferred to play rougher games with her male classmates. A transgender person born male may have wanted to wear feminine and not masculine clothing, and he may have felt trapped in the wrong body.

Many teens may have had feelings like this at one time or another. In fact, most people have occasionally wondered what it would be like to be a member of the opposite sex. Transgender people, however, think about that possibility more frequently, and their feelings are much stronger. They may find that these feelings become

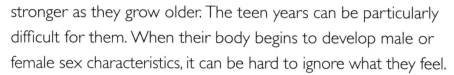
stronger as they grow older. The teen years can be particularly difficult for them. When their body begins to develop male or female sex characteristics, it can be hard to ignore what they feel.

Although they are not sure why yet, experts agree that if you are GLBT, you were born that way. Most experts believe there is a biological basis for sexual orientation. It may be genetic, or it may be based on biological factors in combination with other factors. Whatever the reason, the American Psychological Association, along with many other groups, say you cannot choose to be GLBT—just as straight people didn't choose to be straight. This means you cannot change your sexual orientation.

People who are transgender are not necessarily gay, lesbian, or bisexual. (Although just like a nontransgender person, they might be.) Some transgender people may initially believe they are gay, lesbian, or bisexual. But later, they may realize they are transgender but straight. No one becomes, or chooses to be, transgender. Even though transgender people may be straight, they often identify with the gay, lesbian, and bisexual community. This is because they may have faced many similar life experiences, such as questioning their identity, facing discrimination, or feeling that they just don't fit in.

Thinking Things Through

As you begin to learn about yourself and your sexual identity, there are some stages that you will probably go through. In fact, you may have started going through these stages when you were a young child.

Before you became aware of your sexuality, you may have somehow felt different from other boys or girls. You may have liked to do things that friends of the same sex didn't do. As you've grown older, these feelings may have become more pronounced. Now that you're a teen, you may also be questioning your sexuality because you are attracted to someone of the same sex.

Many experts believe that your genes not only determine whether you are male or female, but also determine your sexual orientation.

It is normal to question your sexual orientation. There's no test you can take to determine if you're GLBT, so it will require some thinking on your part to discover your sexual orientation. Remember, it is all part of figuring out who you are as a person. Don't be afraid to consult resources like the organizations and Web sites listed in the back of this book. Once you've done some reading on this topic, talk to a parent or friend, a doctor, or another adult you trust. Everyone's

Gender Transition for Transgender Teens

Some transgender people decide to go through what is known as gender transition. This means changing their physical appearance to match how they feel on the inside. If a transgender person decides to undergo this transition, he or she can do it in a variety of ways. Some may change their hairstyle, clothing, and name to go along with their gender identity. Some may wear makeup. Others may take hormones to change their secondary sex characteristics. Still others may have surgery to make permanent changes to their primary sex characteristics.

To undergo a full gender transition, you have to be at least eighteen years old, and you'll need to undergo therapy. Doctors usually require that you change your outward physical appearance or secondary sex characteristics first. You must live with those changes for a certain period of time before you can have surgery. Full gender transition is a very serious step and therefore should not be taken lightly.

As a transgender teen, you may want to consider changing your outward appearance to better match how you feel inside. You can do that by changing your hairstyle, your clothing, or your name. Some transgender teens choose to do nothing at all. Only do what you feel comfortable with. Don't let anyone pressure you to make changes that you aren't ready for.

experience of learning that they are GLBT is different. Some people decide to get further help, such as counseling. This can help you make decisions and feel more comfortable about your situation. Ask a parent or check online resources for help finding a counselor specializing in working with GLBT teens.

Deciding to Come Out to Your Friends

If you discover that you are GLBT, you may eventually decide to "come out" to your friends. Coming out is the process of telling the people around you what your real sexual orientation or gender identity is.

There are many things to consider before making the decision to come out to your friends, such as who to come out to and when to do it. There is no reason to rush this process. Think about what you want to accomplish. Preparing to come out can be overwhelming at first because there is so much to think about. It can seem like a scary process. However, keep in mind that you are not the first person to discover that you are GLBT. Many people have had similar experiences, and they can help guide you. Books, reputable Web sites, and support groups can provide plenty of information to help you make good decisions.

While you're thinking about when to come out and to whom, gather as much information as you can. Read about others' coming-out experiences in books, magazines, and online articles. Their experiences will give you things to consider and may offer helpful advice. However, remember that you are unique. Only you can make the decision that is right for you. Try not to feel pressure to come out on anyone else's timetable. Come out when it feels right to you and when you feel comfortable with your sexual identity.

One major thing to consider is timing. If you are in middle school or high school, what is your school like? Are other students tolerant? Or are you afraid you'll be bullied? Are there supportive teachers or counselors you would be able to talk to? Think carefully about your home situation, too. How do you think your family may react? Would your parents and siblings be accepting? Hostile? Do you have people in your life that will support you? Some people decide to come out as soon as they know that they are GLBT, no matter what their present situation. Others may decide to wait until they have graduated from high school or no longer live with their family.

You should also think about whom you want to come out to first. In many cases, people decide to come out to someone they are very close to, such as a best friend, a sibling, or a parent. It's helpful to choose someone you think will be positive about your news so that he or she can support you when you come out to others. Try to get an idea of where that person stands on GLBT issues. Have you heard him or her mention a gay

These teens are attending a summer bible camp for GLBT people in Deerwood, Minnesota. Having a group of supportive peers can be a great help if you are a GLBT teen.

or lesbian friend in a positive way? Has the person made homophobic jokes or statements in the past? If you don't have a good idea of where the person stands, bring up a movie or book with GLBT themes, or discuss a GLBT topic in the news to see what he or she has to say.

If you're unsure of the reaction you may get from your friends, consider coming out to a supportive person who is more neutral. This might include a teacher you trust, a school counselor, or your family doctor.

Another thing to think about when choosing the first person you want to tell is confidentiality. This is an especially important consideration if you're thinking about telling a friend who goes to your school. Do you think the person you've chosen will keep the news to himself or herself? If not, and you're not ready for your classmates to know, you may want to consider waiting or telling someone else.

Consider all the factors mentioned above when deciding whether or not to come out to your friends. Think about why you want to come out, and try to wait until you have a positive reason to do so. An example of a positive reason might be that you want your friends and loved ones to know the real you. If you come out for a negative reason, such as to shock someone, you might not be as happy with your decision in the long run.

You will need to consider the reaction you may get from the person you plan to tell. Some people may be surprised or confused. Others may feel angry or hurt. Some might deny that you are GLBT, or tell you that you're being silly. Still others may have suspected you were GLBT and will be happy that you can now freely discuss your identity.

Most of the time, people will—sooner or later—be supportive and positive about your news. However, you should be prepared in case of a negative reaction. Think about how

There are many ways for GLBT teens to come out to their friends.
This person came out on his blog in 2009.

you might handle a situation where a friend says that he or she doesn't want to be friends with you anymore.

When You're Ready to Come Out

If you've made your decision about when to come out and to whom, you might want to practice what you want to say. You should also try to find a time when you and the person you are telling are relaxed and in a private setting. Blurting out "I'm bisexual!" when you and your mom are in a store or are running late for a school event might be too stressful. In these situations, you probably wouldn't have time for a good discussion. It's better to find a time when you can be alone and talk things through.

After you've told the other person, give him or her some time to think and adjust. Be patient and allow him or her to take in what you've just revealed. Even if the person's first reaction is not positive, it doesn't mean that he or she won't eventually be comfortable with the news. It can take a while for people to adjust. Some people may take weeks—or even years—to get used to the idea. And some people may never truly accept you for who you are. It's important to take rejection in stride, even though it may be difficult. If some people react unreasonably to your coming out, there may be little you can do for them but be patient.

If you're coming out as transgender, the people you tell may not understand at first. If the person doesn't know much about what it means to be transgender, he or she may be confused. People, especially parents, may feel that they did something wrong or that they somehow "made" you transgender. Try to be patient with them, and be prepared with information that can help them understand. There are many resources for families of people who are transgender. Keep in mind that you've had time to think about what it means to be transgender, and they may not have.

Bisexual teens may have a similar problem when coming out: not everyone understands what it means to be bisexual. People may say, "You aren't bisexual. You're just confused." Or they may unfairly accuse you of being promiscuous because you're attracted to people of both sexes. Again, it can help to be patient. And be prepared with information about what it means to be bisexual.

Whether you are gay, lesbian, bisexual, or transgender, it can help to remind the person you're coming out to that you are still the same person you've always been. One of the benefits to coming out is that in most cases your relationship with the other person will improve. You will be able to have a better relationship if you can be who you really are and can openly discuss all aspects of your life. In most cases, your relationship with yourself will improve as well.

However, this will not be true in some cases. Some people will never be accepting, and there is a chance you could lose a friend for good. Unfortunately, some people may react very poorly. They may call you names or threaten to out you to others. These reactions are not the norm, but be prepared. In a hostile situation, try to remain calm and not react in anger. If you cannot reason with the person, leave them alone and let them know you'll try to get in touch in a little while. Let the person have a few days, or even weeks, to process the information. If they still react poorly after some cooldown time, try your best to accept the situation.

Once you have come out, the next phase you may go through is adjusting to your GLBT identity. You may exhibit pride in your GLBT identity and decide to call attention to that aspect of yourself. It may feel that your sexuality is the most important thing about you. Eventually, your identity as a GLBT person becomes just another aspect of who you are. Remember that there is no rush to come out. Go at your own pace, and do it when you feel fully ready.

CHAPTER 2

THE IMPORTANCE OF FRIENDS

When you hear the word "relationship," you may immediately think of a boyfriend or girlfriend. But a relationship isn't just with a romantic partner. A relationship is any ongoing interaction with another person.

Relationships are a valuable part of your life. Your interactions with the people in your life can be an important source of support in your teen years. This is true for anyone, but friendships and relationships can be essential when you are going through a difficult time.

Because relationships are so worthwhile and helpful, it's important to take good care of your friendships. Spend time with your friends when things are going well and when they're not. Listen and be supportive when your friends need you, and they will reward you with the same. Your friends can be some of the most important people in your life, and maintaining a

The teen years can be difficult, and maintaining strong friendships can help you get through them. A good friend will be there to support you when times are tough.

good relationship with them is very important. Spend time with your friends when things are going well and when they're not. Be there for them if they someone to talk to. Listen and be supportive when your friends need you, and they will reward you with the same.

Having GLBT Friends

It's very important to try to find friends who are also GLBT but not romantic partners. They, too, may be questioning their sexual orientation. There is a good chance that they will really know what it's like to face the same things you may be facing as a GLBT teen. Like you, they may be preparing to come out or may have come out recently. Their experiences can allow them to be particularly supportive. For example, GLBT friends might be able to offer help dealing with hostile classmates. They also might be able to give you tips on where to meet other GLBT teens and what support groups or GLBT social groups you could join.

Meeting friends who are GLBT allows you to expand your social circle. You'll meet their friends and their friends' friends. Of course, just because someone is GLBT doesn't automatically mean you will get along with him or her. Just as with meeting and becoming friends with straight people, you'll find some GLBT people with whom you'll connect and others you won't like as much.

Homophobia

Homophobia describes a range of anti-GLBT behaviors. These behaviors can be subtle, such as avoiding or looking down on GLBT people, to overt harassment like name-calling or even physical assault. Homophobia is based on fear or a lack of understanding about GLBT people. If you experience homophobia in any form, keep in mind that it's not your fault. You didn't do anything wrong, and you don't deserve to be treated poorly. Homophobia is the result of other people's ignorance.

This girl attends a 2007 rally in Sacramento, California, against discrimination toward GLBT individuals.

Straight Friends

When you're thinking about coming out, you may be concerned about how your sexual orientation will affect your relationships with straight friends. While it's true that in some cases your relationships will change, in most situations you'll be able to continue your friendships just as they were before. Your openness may actually improve your relationships. Your friend may feel like he or she knows you better now. Or your friend may feel glad that you trusted him or her enough to share such personal information.

Revealing that you are GLBT may change your relationship with some of your straight friends for the worse. They may not feel comfortable because their religious or family background has made them homophobic. Some may worry that you'll try to have a physical relationship with them, even though that is not your intention. Sometimes, you may not be able to overcome their objection to your sexual orientation. But remember that even initial negative reactions may be temporary. Be patient and let your friends get used to the idea. Explain as much as you can about your sexual orientation. Reassure them that the fact that you are GLBT doesn't mean you will try to date your same-sex friends and that you won't try to "turn" them GLBT. Remind them that you're exactly the same person they were friends with before you came out.

In some cases, your friends may not be able to cope with your sexual orientation. Sometimes, there may be little you can

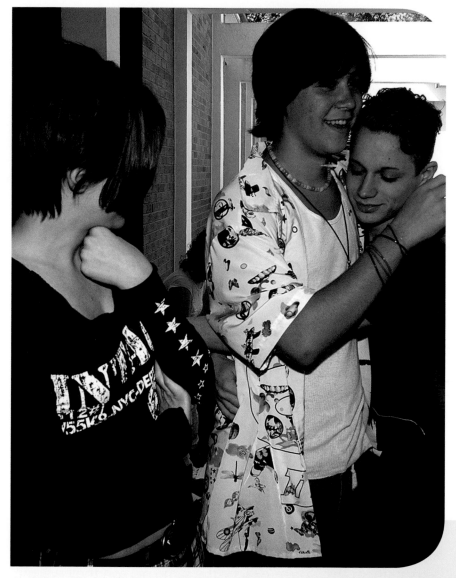

A GSA offers a great chance for students to learn about each other.
Understanding other people's perspectives is an important life skill.
These teens are members of a gay-straight alliance in Decatur, Georgia.

do to make them understand that they are acting unreasonably. If a friendship ends when you come out, it can be very painful. It can be as difficult as when you break up with a romantic partner. Don't be afraid to talk with your other friends, your parents, or other supportive adults if you are having a hard time.

Another thing that may come up after you're out to a straight friend is thinking about how to handle a crush on him or her. Take your time to think about whether or not it makes sense to tell your friend. Would your friend be offended if you told him or her? If you haven't come out, would your friend out you to others if he or she didn't feel comfortable with your feelings? You take a risk any time you reveal an attraction to a friend—GLBT or straight—so be prepared. You just might get a positive reaction, but it also could potentially end the friendship.

Gay-Straight Alliances

A gay-straight alliance (GSA) is a school club where both GLBT and straight students come together to create a safe academic environment for all students. They work to prevent harassment and bullying, and they fight homophobia in school and the surrounding community. Joining a GSA is a great way to meet other out GLBT students at your school and make new straight friends, too. It can also provide a real sense of unity and belonging.

The decision to join a GSA can be difficult for some students. They may fear that they'll be the subject of bullying or abuse. Straight students may worry that people will assume they are GLBT if they join. But joining a GSA is actually one of the best ways to counteract homophobia and bullying. There are currently thousands of GSAs in schools across the country. If your school doesn't already have a GSA, you might want to consider starting one.

To start a GSA, find a supportive teacher or school counselor who can help you by sponsoring the club. Then follow your school's procedure for starting a new club.

CHAPTER 3

GETTING READY TO DATE

When you are a teenager, whether you're GLBT or straight, you may feel pressure to have a girlfriend or boyfriend. Some of your friends may be dating. Or maybe you've seen a movie or television show where all the teens are paired up. This doesn't mean you have to be in a relationship, or even dating. Take your time and begin dating when you feel comfortable.

Are You Ready?

Doing some thinking before you begin dating is a good idea. Consider why you want to date. Is it because everyone else seems to be dating? Or are you bored? Or feeling lonely? None of these are good reasons to jump into dating. You should begin dating when you are comfortable with who you are and when you find someone who you want to spend time with.

Participating in group activities can be a great way to ease into dating. You can get to know other people and have fun interacting with your peers, whether they are GLBT or straight.

If you don't feel ready to date right now, it doesn't mean you won't feel ready in a month or in a year. Just be patient. You'll only feel more stress if you push yourself to do something that you're not ready for. Even if you don't feel ready to date, you can still have fun in a group setting. It's important to hang out with your friends. And doing something active with several people can be a good way to get to know others.

Meeting Other GLBT Teens

Once you've decided that you are ready to date, you'll need to meet other GLBT teens in your area. The good news is that it's becoming easier for GLBT teens to meet each other. Society is changing its views on people who are GLBT. As a result, more teens feel comfortable coming out and being open about their sexual identity.

GLBT resource centers, such as this one at the University of California, Irvine, can be an important source of information for GLBT teens.

One good way to meet other GLBT teens is through local organizations and support groups. A GSA at your school is one type of organization where you may meet other teens that are open to dating. Joining groups like GLBT teen support groups outside of school can allow you to meet other teens that don't go to your school but may live nearby. These groups often host social events, especially for teens.

Local shops like bookstores or coffeehouses may host events for GLBT teens. Check local newspapers or Web sites to find teen events in your neighborhood. Some towns and cities also have teen nightclubs and other venues for people who are under twenty-one, or they will host weekly or monthly events for underage people. Some of these nightclubs have regularly scheduled events for GLBT teens.

Another easy way to meet other GLBT teens is through online chat rooms or support groups. Meeting people online can be a simple way to get to know someone. You can find people with common interests and backgrounds, and you can learn from each other's experiences as GLBT teens. You can get instant feedback and support, and you can even offer feedback and support to others. Because you can communicate anonymously, you may feel more comfortable discussing certain things than you would with someone you know. However, it's important to proceed with caution. There are risks to interacting online, so it is essential that you guard your privacy and personal information. See the Online Safety section on page 57 for more information.

How Do You Know If Someone Is GLBT?

Maybe you met someone interesting at your sister's soccer game. You really hit it off but aren't sure if he or she is straight or GLBT. How can you tell? GLBT people don't wear a nametag that states their sexual orientation. And it's usually not best to ask outright. Think about how you might react if

Same-Sex Marriages

Many GLBT people are in long-term relationships and want to make the lasting commitment of marriage. For GLBT people, getting married formalizes their partnership in their eyes and in the eyes of society. Being married also gives a couple legal benefits, such as joint tax filing and the right to visit a spouse in the intensive care unit of a hospital.

In most U.S. states, marriage is not recognized legally for GLBT couples. However, that's changing. A growing number of states give GLBT couples the right to get married. Other states allow civil unions, which provide GLBT couples with some legal benefits as partners. However, same-sex marriages and civil unions are not recognized at the federal level of government. In some countries, same-sex marriage is legal. For instance, Canada legalized same-sex marriage nationwide with the Civil Marriage Act of 2005.

This couple returns from their wedding in June 2008. Several U.S. states now recognize same-sex marriages.

someone you just met immediately asked you to state your sexual orientation.

One way to find out is to drop casual hints in the conversation about your own sexual orientation. For instance, you could mention an event you attended at a GLBT teen club or a GLBT school organization that you belong to. If the person doesn't give you any hints in return, he or she may not have picked up on your clues. You can try dropping more hints, or if you feel comfortable, go ahead and ask directly. A better strategy would be to ask friends, peers, and teachers you can trust if they know that the person is GLBT.

Don't worry if it turns out that the other person is not GLBT. If you make light of the situation, the other person probably will, too. If the other person is GLBT but isn't interested in dating you, try not to take it too hard. Being rejected is simply part of dating.

However, be aware that some teens may take offense if you assume that they are GLBT. It's possible that they will react badly and perhaps even threaten you. If this happens, it's important to stay calm. If you also react badly, it might just make the situation worse. Explain that you made an incorrect assumption and that you didn't mean to offend him or her. If this does not defuse the situation, don't be afraid to ask an adult for help.

In most cases, the situation will not be this extreme. Use your judgment, and don't let the possibility of being rejected deter you. Putting yourself out there is difficult, but take a chance.

CHAPTER 4

Dating

Dating can be difficult and scary, but it can also be fun and rewarding. This is true for every teen, both GLBT and straight. In some ways, dating as a GLBT teen may be easier than for a straight teen. In other ways, it may be more difficult. But it may not be that different at all.

Society has set fewer "rules" regarding dating for GLBT teens. On the other hand, straight teens have many models for what dating "should" be like. Maybe their parents or older siblings have told them what to expect. Or they've seen depictions of teens dating on television. GLBT teens see fewer role models in the media and in society in general. Some see this lack of rules and expectations as an advantage. It can mean you are free to create a relationship that feels right for you.

As a GLBT teen, you may not know what to expect when you're ready to date. You may wonder how or where you'll

Sometimes, dating can lead to a committed relationship. Be sure that you date people that you like and respect, rather than people your friends might pressure you to date.

meet other GLBT teens. You may not be sure what kind of relationship you'll have with someone you're dating or how to handle things if one or both of you aren't out to friends and classmates.

GLBT teens often have fewer options when it comes to the people they can date. Statistically, there are just fewer GLBT teens than straight teens, and some GLBT teens are still discovering who they are. Although you may not have as many dating options as your straight peers, don't succumb to pressure from yourself or from anyone else to date someone solely because he or she is GLBT. You should date someone because you like, respect, and are attracted to each other and have common interests.

Asking Someone on a Date

One traditional custom of straight dating used to be that the man asked the woman to go on a date. He also paid for the date. This rule is no longer strictly observed. Now many

A teenage couple walks down Martin Luther King Jr. Boulevard in Newark, New Jersey. At the time this photograph was taken, they had been together for two years.

women ask men out, and there aren't any set rules as to who has to pay. The same is true for GLBT teens: either person should feel free to invite a prospective partner to go out. And there are no set rules about who should pay. Sometimes, people choose to split the costs. Other times, the person who did the asking will do the paying. Some people take turns paying. Do whatever works for you and your date.

Your First GLBT Relationship

Your first GLBT relationship may be wonderful. It can be fun to get to know someone else and get to know yourself better in the process. But a first relationship (or a second relationship, or even a tenth relationship) can be confusing. Maybe your partner is out and you're not. Or maybe your partner has had more experience dating than you have. Sometimes, a relationship may be risky for one partner because of family, religious, or school reasons. This can be unfortunate, but it's not necessarily unusual. Some of these issues can come up in straight relationships, too.

If you are experiencing any of these issues with a person you are with, take it slow. Be sure to talk to your partner about any problems. Sometimes, the other person may not see the situation as a problem, or he or she may have a completely different take on the situation. Make your feelings and opinions known so that the other person understands where you're coming from. Maintain good relationships with your friends so that you'll have a strong support system. Take time away from dating to do other things that you enjoy. This will help ensure that you maintain your own identity—one that is separate from your relationship with the person you're dating.

Cross-Cultural Dating

As a GLBT teen, you may be well aware that some people can be intolerant of other people's sexual orientation. You're probably also aware that there are people who are not tolerant of people of different racial or religious backgrounds. If you date someone of a different race or religion, you may encounter intolerance from friends or family—or even from people in your community. This can be intimidating and may present extra challenges, but it doesn't have to be an impossible situation.

One thing that you can try to do is help others learn to be more tolerant. You can't expect someone to change his or her views overnight, but you may make progress over time. Even though it may be difficult, try to have relaxed discussions instead of screaming matches. Let them get to know your partner and learn who he or she is as a person. Some people are intolerant because they have never actually gotten to know a member of the group that they're prejudiced against. The key is to be patient.

You can also try joining a support group for people in cross-cultural relationships. Look online for resources, and try to meet others who are in similar relationships. They may be able to give advice on how to handle certain situations.

Dating Safety

Most of the time, dating can be a lot of fun. But as a GLBT teen, there are some things that you should watch out for. Public displays of affection (PDA) between straight partners are often considered to be socially acceptable—provided they don't go too far. Therefore, PDA should be socially acceptable for GLBT partners as well, but that's not necessarily the case. Not all people are tolerant, and some might express their lack of tolerance with verbal or physical abuse. Use your best judgment, trust your instincts, and be cautious. If you and your date are kissing in public and you see someone staring at you in a threatening manner, you may want to wait and express your affection when you're in a safer environment.

You should also be careful of where you go on a date with someone you don't yet know well. When going on a first date, only agree to meet in a public place or a location where you know there will be other people around. Tell someone where you're going and when you plan to be back.

A "Cure" for Being GLBT?

Some people believe you can change your sexual orientation. There are groups that say they can "cure" people who are homosexual. They claim to be able to do this through religion, therapy, or a combination of both. However, just as it is not possible to change other inborn traits, you cannot change your sexual orientation. It's possible to change your behavior, just as it's possible to change or cover up other inborn traits. For instance, if you have brown hair, you could dye it blond. But that wouldn't change the fact that you were born with brown hair. If you are a lesbian, you could behave as though you aren't—for instance, you could date men. But by dating someone of the opposite sex, you haven't changed the underlying fact that you are a lesbian.

Some gay people make an effort to ignore their sexual orientation. A few individuals will even marry people of the opposite sex, or have children with them, in an attempt to conform to what they believe their friends, family's, or culture's expectations are for how they should behave. While they may fool people into thinking that they are straight, or even fool themselves, they ultimately cannot change their sexual orientation.

Are You Ready to Have Sex?

Having a sexual relationship can be a component of dating, but it is not a requirement of dating. Even if you feel that you are in

love with your partner, it doesn't mean you will automatically be ready for sex. Love and sex are two very different things. Keep in mind that there are many nonsexual ways to express your love, such as kissing, cuddling, or holding hands. Plenty of teens date without having sex. And many teens who say they are having sex actually may not be—they just want you to think they are. It may be hard to avoid feeling pressure to have sex from peers, from your partner, or even from movies and television. Even so, don't have sex just because everyone else is. You're the only one who can make the decision that's right for you.

As a teenager, your body is biologically prepared for sex, but that doesn't mean your mind is ready. There are a lot of things to think about when deciding if you're ready to have sex, so take your time. Ask yourself questions when you're trying to make your decision. For example: Am I ready for sex, and if so, why? What does sex mean to me? What does sex include? What kind of relationship do I want to be in before I'm ready? What are my family's values about sex? What are my religious beliefs concerning sex?

Get as much information as you can to help you make your decision. As a GLBT teen, you may have to work a little harder to find information that pertains to you. When sex is discussed by parents or in health classes, it's usually geared toward heterosexuals. However, there is good information available for GLBT teens. Use your health teacher, school counselor, or a teen GLBT organization as a resource. Your school or public library

This transgender teen is biologically female but identifies as male.
He was elected as a candidate for prom king of his Fresno, California,
high school in 2007.

will likely have books containing excellent, in-depth information
to help you make your decision. See the For Further Reading
and For More Information sections of this book for more
resources.

While dating may help you figure out your sexual
orientation, having sex will not. Being intimate with someone of

It's important to educate yourself about sex before you begin a sexual relationship. Read about it, think about it, and talk things through with teachers, counselors, and your partner to be sure that you're ready.

the same or opposite sex is only one piece of who you are. A sexual encounter will not "prove" one way or the other if you are GLBT.

If you do decide to have sex, prepare yourself ahead of time and be sure to have safe sex. Remember, if you do have sex and it doesn't feel comfortable to you, trust your instincts and stop. There is absolutely no reason why you can't wait until you are ready. If the person you are dating deserves your attention, he or she will respect your decision.

Sexually Transmitted Diseases and Pregnancy

If you are sexually active, sexually transmitted diseases (STDs) and pregnancy are possible consequences. STDs are diseases that can be passed from one person to another through contact with bodily fluids during sex. Some examples of STDs are gonorrhea, herpes, human immunodeficiency virus (HIV), and syphilis. Learn about these diseases and how they are spread before you begin a sexual relationship. STDs can be very serious. The only way to completely protect yourself from getting one is to abstain from having sex. However, if you are sexually active, you can reduce your chances of getting STDs by practicing safer sex. Using condoms and dental dams can help you protect yourself from STDs.

If you haven't already learned about STDs in a health class at school, go to a school or public library to get more information about how to protect yourself from them. You might also want to talk to your doctor.

As with STDs, there is only one surefire way to keep from getting pregnant: not having sex. But if you are sexually active with a partner of the opposite sex, always use a condom. You may want to use another form of birth control in addition to a condom. Educate yourself about preventing pregnancy before you become sexually active.

Meeting Your Partner's Friends and Family

Part of getting to know another person in a dating relationship is meeting their friends and family. However, if you are in a

Some GLBT people's families are very supportive, such as these families marching at the St. Louis, Missouri, 2005 PrideFest parade.

GLBT relationship, you may not always get that chance—or at least not right away. Sometimes, your partner may not be out to his or her family or friends. If that's the case, your partner may ask that you act a certain way around them, or maybe not meet them at all. This may be disappointing, but it's important to be supportive and respect your partner's wishes. He or she has the right to come out when ready, not on a timetable you've set. Just because you can't meet your partner's friends or family right away doesn't mean you won't be able to in the future.

CHAPTER 5

Dating Pitfalls

Although dating can be fun and exciting, it is not without risks. You should know what to watch out for in your relationships and what kind of behavior is unacceptable. Cheating and jealousy can be dating pitfalls that you'll want to try to avoid. You should also know what to be aware of if you are thinking of dating someone older or someone you met online. You should know to look out for abusive behavior from a partner. You should also be careful not to act in an abusive manner toward your partner.

Cheating and Jealousy

Mild forms of jealousy are a natural part of a relationship. In most cases, a partner who is jealous simply feels insecure. If your partner feels jealous, try to reassure him or her. If you are

It's important to respect the person you are dating and to be open and honest with him or her.

feeling jealous, be sure to talk to your partner about it. Be honest, but be reasonable: Don't expect your partner to spend all his or her time with you, or never talk to other people. Extreme forms of jealousy, such as trying to prevent you from spending time with friends, can be a form of abuse. Remember that you don't deserve abuse and do not have to tolerate it.

Cheating can be hard to define. Some people consider kissing someone outside your relationship cheating. Other people might think that only having sex with someone else is cheating. Make sure you and your partner have the same idea about what is and isn't cheating. Once you've defined your rules, respect them.

If your partner cheats on you, it is not your fault. It is not the result of something you did or didn't do. You will need to make your own decision about whether to break up or try to work things out. Remember that, as with abuse, you do not deserve to be cheated on. If you cheat on your partner, you need to be honest with him or her about it. If you are unhappy with your relationship, you should break up with your partner rather than hurting him or her even more.

Dating an Older Partner

Dating a partner who is older than you may seem exciting. Older partners may seem like they know more than you do, and they may be able to do things you're not allowed to yet, such as drive a car. Maybe they've been "out" longer or have more dating experience. Because they've been through what you've been through as a GLBT teen, they may be able to offer advice and support.

An older partner may be dating you because he or she likes and respects you. However, it's also quite possible that the person is trying to take advantage of someone who is younger and less knowledgeable. Older partners may be dating you because they feel they'll have power over you. They may also be dating you in the hopes that you'll do things they ask without questioning, such as participating in risky sex.

You may have your own reasons for dating an older partner. Some reasons may be good, and others may be not as good. Dating an older partner to impress your friends or have someone take care of you are not good reasons.

If you are dating an older partner, first, make sure you are doing it for the right reasons. Make sure to take your time. Move at a pace that is comfortable for you. Don't let your partner force you to do things that you don't want to do. Watch out for an older partner—or any partner—who wants to keep your relationship with them secret or doesn't want you to tell anyone that the two of you are dating. Another warning sign is a partner who refuses to meet your friends and family, or won't let you meet theirs. Yet another warning sign is a partner who wants to keep you away from your family, friends, and school commitments. If you don't feel comfortable, tell someone—a parent, friend, counselor, teacher, or another adult that you trust—about the relationship.

While in some cases it may be OK to date an older partner, it's never all right to date a teacher, a coach, or an adult friend of your family. If a school official or family friend tries to date you, let someone know.

Myths and Facts

Myth: A person can choose whether or not to be GLBT.

Fact: No one can choose his or her sexuality. Just as you are born with blue, brown, or green eyes, you are born straight, gay, lesbian, bisexual, or transgender.

Myth: GLBT people don't have "normal" relationships.

Fact: Every relationship is different, but GLBT people can and do have the same kinds of relationships that straight people do. Some GLBT couples have loving long-term relationships. And just as is true of straight couples, some GLBT couples' relationships are not perfect.

Myth: Bisexual people are actually gay or lesbian and are just confused about their sexuality.

Fact: It's true that some people who identify as bisexual are experimenting to come to a better understanding of who they are. Some may eventually decide that they are gay or lesbian or straight. However, others are truly sexually attracted to people of both sexes.

The Internet can be a great place for GLBT teens to get information and meet people. However, some people use the Internet to target GLBT teens for harassment and bullying.

Online Safety

As we've discussed, the Internet can be a great place to meet other GLBT teens and get information about GLBT issues. There are many advantages to the Internet, but there are also many things that you should watch out for.

If you are getting information on a GLBT topic from the Internet, make sure to check the source of the information. Does a reputable organization sponsor the site? Can you find similar information on other sites as well? If you have to register to use a Web site, only give a user name and password. Don't use your real name, and don't give out any personal information like your address or phone number.

When interacting with someone online, be cautious. The other person may not be honest with you about who he or she is. It is very easy to pretend to be someone you're not online. You can pretend to

If you're in an abusive relationship, tell someone you trust. It may be a difficult conversation to have, but you may need support to get out of—and get over—an abusive relationship.

be older, younger, thinner, or richer than you really are. But just because you can doesn't mean you should. Watch out for someone whose personal details don't add up.

You should be cautious about anyone who asks you to reveal personal details about your life right away. Under no circumstances should you send them photos of yourself, your friends, or your family. There is no way for you to know where these photos and other personal information will end up.

Avoid becoming too heavily involved with a person online or becoming dependent on his or her support. Because you don't know who the person really is, it's best not to get too emotionally invested in that person. After all, it's possible that one day that person may just stop communicating with you.

Don't agree to meet someone you've met online unless your parents have agreed to it. If you're not yet out to your parents, tell another trusted adult. It's important that you only agree to meet in a safe, public location. It's also important to bring a friend, sibling, or other trusted person along with you.

Abusive Relationships

Much of the time, having a relationship with another person can be positive and rewarding. Unfortunately, not all relationship experiences are positive. A bad relationship might include physical, emotional, or even sexual abuse. Emotional abuse can include insults or name-calling, controlling behavior, jealousy, possessiveness, or threats. In GLBT relationships, this might include threatening to out a partner who has not revealed his or her sexual orientation to family and friends. Hitting, slapping, punching, kicking, biting, and throwing things are all examples of physical abuse. Sexual abuse can include forcing a partner to have sex when he or she is not ready or does not want to have sex. In addition to these types of behavior, abusive partners may try to keep you away from your family, friends, and other sources of support. It's important that you do not allow anyone you are dating to isolate you from the people you love and trust.

Abusive partners often try to make it up to you after the abuse. They may promise that it will never happen again. In nearly all cases, however, it will. If you are in a relationship that includes abusive behavior, here are some things to think about. First of all, you do not deserve to be abused. The abuse is not your fault, even if your partner says it is. People who abuse are doing it to gain power over you, plain and simple.

You have two options if you are in an abusive relationship. You can try to change things, or you can break up. You may want to try talking to your partner about the abuse and how it makes you feel. Depending on his or her response, you can decide whether or not to give your partner another chance. But know that the abuse may very well happen again. Remember, you do not deserve the abuse. Get counseling for yourself, or call a crisis hotline for help. Talk to your parents or a counselor at school about the problem. You don't need to deal with this problem alone.

CHAPTER 6
When a Relationship Ends

A breakup can be painful and confusing, but sometimes it's necessary to end a relationship. There are several reasons why you may want or need to break up with someone. If your partner is abusive or controlling, you should end the relationship. If you can't be open and honest with your partner, or you feel your partner isn't being honest with you, you may want to consider breaking up. A breakup may be necessary if your partner expects you to change who you are to get his or her acceptance or approval. The pressure from one partner to come out to others can cause a breakup. Or, people may simply break up because they are no longer attracted to each other or aren't interested in the same things.

Breakups are rarely easy, but try to remember that you once both cared about each other. Be as kind as you can to your partner, and yourself, when going through a breakup.

How to Break Up

Breakups can be sudden or gradual. They can be sudden if you find out that your partner has cheated on you, for example. Or you may want to make a quick, clean break if you are in an abusive relationship, your partner is very possessive, or is threatening to out you before you are ready. Under these circumstances, make it clear to your partner that it is over. Explain that you won't be able to see him or her or talk on the phone or e-mail. Then stand your ground.

It is important to talk to the people you are closest with about breaking up with your partner. Let your friends and family know about the decision so that they can support you and back you up. If you are not out to all your friends or family, try to talk to someone who knows about the relationship so that he or she can help you through the situation. Whatever you do, don't try to go through a breakup alone.

In other situations, breaking up might be a gradual process. If you and your partner are having trouble working out disagreements that you've been having for a long time, you may want to start discussing the possibility of a breakup. This can give both people a chance to get used to the idea. It can also help you figure out if there's a chance to keep the relationship going.

Ten Great Questions to Ask a School Guidance Counselor

1. How can I tell if I'm **GLBT**?

2. Can you change whether or not you're **GLBT**?

3. How do I tell my friends and family that I'm **GLBT**?

4. What should I do if my friends react negatively to the fact that I'm **GLBT**?

5. How can I tell if someone I'm interested in is **GLBT**?

6. Where can I meet other **GLBT** teens?

7. Will having sex help me decide if I am **GLBT**?

8. What should I do if the person I'm dating pressures me to come out to my friends?

9. What should I do if my partner's family doesn't accept me?

10. Who can I talk to about a breakup if I have not come out to my family or friends?

Surviving a Breakup

Ending a relationship can often be heartbreaking and confusing. This is especially true if your partner has broken up with you. The bad news is that there's no magic pill to take to make breaking up hurt less. The good news is that, eventually, you will feel better.

Everyone, and every breakup, is different. No matter who you are, you will need some time to get over the anger and sadness that you may feel. It's natural to feel upset, so it can be a good idea to discuss your feelings with someone. You can also write about your feelings in a journal or talk to a counselor. Do whatever makes you feel better: cry, scream, talk with friends, go for a run, or bake a cake. Do active things that will take your mind off of your situation for a while. Take up a new hobby or work on an old hobby, help a friend with his or her homework, join a club or GLBT support group, take a road trip with your mom, or do something nice for your grandfather.

Don't ignore the feelings of sadness, confusion, or anger that you may have. You need to give yourself time to work through them. But try not to let your negative feelings overwhelm you. While you're going through a breakup, you may feel depressed, but don't forget to take good care of yourself. Try to get your normal amount of sleep and eat well. Exercise is one thing that can help you feel better. Know that it might take a little while

Part of being a teenager is experiencing a lot of emotions, not all of them pleasant. Be sure to ask a parent, teacher, or counselor for help if you are having trouble dealing with your feelings.

for you to feel like yourself again. It may take a week or a month—or even longer. No matter how long it takes, you will eventually feel better. And someday, you will find someone new to date.

However, if you aren't starting to feel better in a month or two, you may be suffering from depression. Depression can be common after a breakup, and it's very common for teens. GLBT teens can be especially susceptible to depression because their lives are sometimes more complicated than the lives of straight teens. Remember, feeling down after a breakup is completely normal, but if you find that you are not able to cope with your feelings, ask for help. Talk to a sibling, friend, parent, or someone else you trust. Find a school counselor or an outside counselor with experience working with GLBT teens and who can ensure that counseling will be confidential. Be honest about what you're going through so that the person can help you.

If you have thoughts of hurting yourself, talk to someone right away. Call a suicide prevention hotline or someone who can get help for you, such as a doctor. You should also get help for yourself if you have been abusing alcohol or drugs, or if you have been cutting yourself. Thoughts about harming your ex-partner are another sign that you should talk to someone who can help. See the For More Information section at the back of this book for organizations that can help and for suicide prevention resources.

Relationships come with some ups and downs, but falling in love can be a wonderful thing. Learn to take the good with the bad, and work together to create a happy, healthy relationship.

If you are a GLBT teen who is not out to your friends or family, a breakup can be even more difficult. You may feel that you have to hide your sadness. Or if you aren't able to hide your feelings, your family or friends may wonder why you seem so sad. If you're not out to your family, lean on your friends or join a support group. Don't try to go through your painful feelings alone.

After a Breakup

When you've made it through the initial pain and sadness of a breakup, you may decide to try and be friends with your ex-partner. It can be difficult to be friends with an ex-partner. And in most situations, it takes time. You're not likely to be ready to be friends just a few days, or even a few weeks, after your breakup. Give yourself and your partner time to adjust to the "rules" of a just-friends relationship.

You may want to jump right into a new relationship to take your mind off of your breakup or to feel less lonely. However, you probably won't achieve either of those by getting involved with someone new right away. Try to give yourself time to get over your last relationship before starting a new one. If you manage to meet someone great soon after a breakup and think you want to date, be honest with that person. Explain that you are getting over a relationship, and you want to take things slow. If the person is worth your time, he or she will respect your wishes.

GLOSSARY

bisexual A sexual orientation describing attraction to both males and females.

condom A device, usually made of latex, that is worn over the penis during sexual intercourse to help prevent pregnancy and sexually transmitted diseases.

dental dam A device, usually made of latex, which can be used to reduce the risk of sexually transmitted diseases during oral sex.

discrimination Treating some people better or worse based on certain characteristics, such as their race, gender, or sexual orientation.

gay A term used to describe men who are attracted to other men. It can also be used to describe anyone who is attracted to members of the same sex.

gonorrhea A contagious, sexually transmitted disease of the genital and urinary organs.

harass To create an unpleasant situation through verbal or physical acts.

herpes A virus that can infect the mouth and reproductive organs; it can be transmitted through sexual contact.

HIV Human immunodeficiency virus, which can be sexually transmitted. HIV weakens the body's ability to fight disease and can cause acquired immunodeficiency syndrome (AIDS).

identity The qualities that make one person different from another.

lesbian A term used to describe women who feel romantic and sexual attraction to other women.

orientation A person's identification as to his or her sexual nature.

primary sex characteristics The sexual organs.

secondary sex characteristics Traits related to what biological sex a person is. For instance, male secondary sex characteristics include an Adam's apple and facial hair, and female secondary sex characteristics include breasts and a general lack of facial hair.

sexually transmitted diseases Diseases that are passed from one person to another through contact with bodily fluids during sexual intercourse; also known as STDs.

syphilis A contagious, sexually transmitted disease that can produce rashes and open sores if left untreated.

transgender A term used to describe a person whose biological sex is different from his or her gender.

For More
INFORMATION

AlterHeros

C.P. 476, succursale "C"

Montréal, Québec H2L 4K4

Canada

(514) 846-1398

Web site: http://www.alterheros.com

This bilingual Canadian organization informs and educates teens and their families on GLBT issues.

Canadian Rainbow Health Coalition

P.O. Box 3043

Saskatoon, SK S7K 3S9

Canada

(800) 955-5129

Web site: http://www.rainbowhealth.ca

This organization is devoted to addressing health and wellness issues specific to GLBT individuals.

Gay, Lesbian, and Straight Education
Network (GLSEN)

90 Broad Street, 2nd Floor

New York, NY 10004

(212) 727-0135

Web site: http://www.glsen.org
GLSEN is a national organization that works to help make all students safe in school. GLSEN's Web site includes information on how to start a GSA.

Human Rights Campaign

1640 Rhode Island Avenue

Washington, DC 20036-3278

(800) 777-4723

Web site: http://www.hrc.org
HRC is America's largest civil rights organization striving to achieve lesbian, gay, bisexual, and transgender equality.

Parents, Families, and Friends of Lesbians and Gays (PFLAG)

1726 M Street NW, Suite 400

Washington, DC 20036

(202) 467-8180

Web site: http://community.pflag.org
PFLAG supports, educates, and advocates for GLBT people and their families and friends. Although it is a national group, many areas have a local chapter.

TransYouth Family Allies, Inc.

P.O. Box 1471

Holland, MI 49422

(888) 462-8932

Web site: http://www.imatyfa.org
This group of parents, family, and friends educates others on behalf of transgender youth.

The Trevor Project

9056 Santa Monica Boulevard, Suite 208

West Hollywood, CA 90069

(310) 271-8845

Web site: http://www.thetrevorproject.org

The Trevor Project is a national, around-the-clock crisis and suicide prevention help line for GLBT youth. Its Web site has a forum for questions and a blog about GLBT issues.

Youth Resource

A Project of Advocates for Youth

2000 M Street NW, Suite 750

Washington, DC 20036

(202) 419-3420, ext. 30

Web site: http://www.youthresource.com

Youth Resource is a Web site created by and for GLBT young people that addresses many issues, especially sexual health.

Web Sites

Due to the changing nature of Internet links, Rosen Publishing has developed an online list of Web sites related to the subject of this book. This site is updated regularly. Please use this link to access this list:

http://www.rosenlinks.com/glbt/frie

For Further READING

Garden, Nancy. *Hear Us Out! Lesbian and Gay Stories of Struggles, Progress, and Hope: 1950 to the Present.* New York, NY: Farrar, Straus, and Giroux, 2007.

Huegel, Kelly. *GLBTQ: The Survival Guide for Queer and Questioning Teens.* Minneapolis, MN: Free Spirit Publishing, 2003.

Levithan, David, and Billy Merrell, eds. *The Full Spectrum: A New Generation of Writing About Gay, Lesbian, Bisexual, Transgender, Questioning, and Other Identities.* New York, NY: Alfred A. Knopf, 2006.

Macgillivray, Ian K. *Gay-Straight Alliances: A Handbook for Students, Educators, and Parents.* New York, NY: Harrington Park Press, 2007.

Marcus, Eric. *What If Someone I Know Is Gay?* New York, NY: Simon Pulse, 2007.

Papademetriou, Lisa, and Chris Tebbetts. *M or F?* New York, NY: Razorbill, 2005.

Pardes, Bronwen. *Doing It Right: Making Smart, Safe, and Satisfying Choices About Sex.* New York, NY: Simon Pulse, 2007.

Peters, Julie Ann. *Luna.* New York, NY: Little, Brown Young Readers, 2004.

Wittlinger, Ellen. *Parrotfish.* New York, NY: Simon & Schuster Books for Young Readers, 2007.

BIBLIOGRAPHY

Corinna, Heather. *S.E.X. The All-You-Need-to-Know Guide to Get You Through High School and College.* New York, NY: Marlowe & Company, 2007.

Huegel, Kelly. *GLBTQ: The Survival Guide for Queer and Questioning Teens.* Minneapolis, MN: Free Spirit Publishing, 2003.

Jennings, Kevin, with Pat Shapiro. *Always My Child: A Parent's Guide to Understanding Your Gay, Lesbian, Bisexual, Transgendered, or Questioning Son or Daughter.* New York, NY: Simon & Schuster, 2003.

Macgillivray, Ian K. *Gay-Straight Alliances: A Handbook for Students, Educators, and Parents.* New York, NY: Harrington Park Press, 2007.

Marcus, Eric. *What If Someone I Know Is Gay?* New York, NY: Simon Pulse, 2007.

Pardes, Bronwen. *Doing It Right: Making Smart, Safe, and Satisfying Choices About Sex.* New York, NY: Simon Pulse, 2007.

INDEX

About the Author

Simone Payment has a degree in psychology from Cornell University and a master's degree in elementary education from Wheelock College. She is the author of twenty-two books for young adults. Her book *Inside Special Operations: Navy SEALs* (also from Rosen Publishing) won a 2004 Quick Picks for Reluctant Young Readers award from the American Library Association and is on the Nonfiction Honor List of Voice of Youth Advocates.

Photo Credits

Cover, p. 52 Queerstock.com; cover (inset) © www.istockphoto.com/Brasil2; cover (background and border), pp. 1, 4, 30–31, 56–57, 66 Shutterstock.com; pp. 8–9, 15, 22, 24, 45, 49 © AP Images; p. 11 © Victor Habbick Visions/Photo Researchers, Inc.; p. 17 Newscom; p. 26 © Robin Nelson/PhotoEdit; p. 32 © GIPhotostock/Photo Researchers, Inc.; p. 34 Justin Sullivan/Getty Images; p. 37 © www.istockphoto.com/Simon Zupan; pp. 38–39 Star-Ledger Photographs © The Star-Ledger, Newark, NJ; pp. 46–47 © Spencer Grant/PhotoEdit; p. 58 © Philippe Garo/Photo Researchers, Inc.; p. 62 © David Young-Wolff/PhotoEdit; pp. 68–69 © Rachel Epstein/PhotoEdit.

Designer: Les Kanturek; Photo Researcher: Cindy Reiman